Thor Heyerdahl's Incredible Raft

by Johanna Biviano

Scott Foresman
is an imprint of

Glenview, Illinois • Boston, Massachusetts • Chandler, Arizona
Upper Saddle River, New Jersey

ISBN 13: 978-0-328-51674-2
ISBN 10:   0-328-51674-0

3 4 5 6 7 8 9 10 V0N4 13 12 11 10

An Idea Is Born

A young man from Norway and his wife sit on the beach of Fatu Hiva, a tropical island in French Polynesia, in the Pacific Ocean, northeast of Australia. They dig their feet into the cooling sand, feel the wind, and watch the waves. The young man stares into the horizon. Both wind and waves always come here from the east he notes. He wonders about the first people who came to this island. Suddenly, he gets a remarkable idea.

Thor Heyerdahl and his wife, Liv, first went to Fatu Hiva in 1936. They went to study zoology—the branch of biology that studies animals and animal life—and to collect samples of wildlife. While they were there, Thor also became interested in ancient rock carvings and the myths

about them. These stories told how people first came to the islands of Polynesia.

Thor was sure that the accepted stories and myths about where the Polynesians came from were not correct. Now he had only to prove it.

A traditional Polynesian tiki sculpture

3

Where Did the Polynesians Come from?

There were lots of different theories about where the Polynesians came from. Everyone seemed to have a different idea.

Some anthropologists thought that these people came from the west. They thought Polynesians came originally from India, China, Malaysia—even Germany or Scandinavia! The Polynesians themselves said that their ancestors arrived on the islands after a long journey over the sea.

Thor Heyerdahl was among those who believed that Polynesians may have come from South America. Spanish conquistadores, explorers of the fifteenth and sixteenth centuries, had noted that the native people used small rafts to fish and travel up and down the coast of Peru in South America. If any group of people had traveled to Polynesia 1,000 years before that, they would have used similar small rafts.

How could a tiny raft make a journey of more than 4,000 miles? Everyone thought that a raft made of light balsa wood and handmade rope would never be able to complete the journey.

Or could it? Thor Heyerdahl thought about how similar the pyramids and temples in Polynesia were to buildings found on the coast of Peru. *Could there be a connection?* he wondered.

A Moai figure on Easter Island

Tall Tales or Truth?

Heyerdahl also knew that the conquistadores had heard legends of a bearded, light-skinned people living in Peru, who were led by a man called Kon-Tiki, or the Son of the Sun. Legend had it that these people worshipped a sun god and were later driven out of Peru by the Incas.

Heyerdahl wrote about Spanish explorers finding the South Sea Islands and about how they were astonished to find people of lighter skin with long beards living there. These people claimed that Tiki had brought them to these islands. Could these people be the tribe that had been driven out of Peru?

Thor Heyerdahl thought so. He studied the ocean currents and trade winds of the Pacific Ocean to prove that Polynesians could have made a 4,000-mile journey across that ocean. When he put all the clues together he was sure he had proof that Polynesians could have come from South America. But no one would read his paper or listen to his ideas.

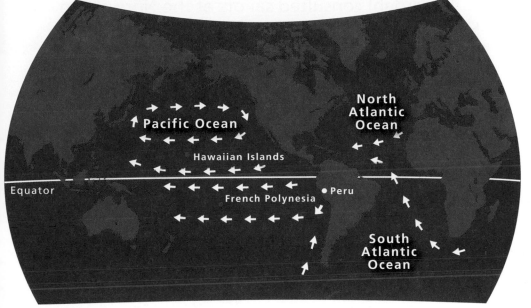

Currents in the Atlantic and Pacific Oceans

The Impossible Adventure

The cooler air and currents from the south flow toward the warmth of the equator. Heyerdahl imagined the mysterious bearded men of Peru floating on a current all the way to Easter Island, Fatu Hiva, and the other islands of Polynesia. He knew that if he could get help to build a raft, he could prove his theory by making the dangerous trip himself!

To make a trip across 4,000 miles of empty ocean, Heyerdahl needed money, supplies, shipmates, and lots of support. He went to New York City to try to convince dignified scholars, seamen, and members of the Explorers Club that his plan would work. Most discouraged him, but one man from the Explorers Club promised to raise money for the adventure.

Heyerdahl Gets Going

Heyerdahl consulted sailors at the Norwegian Sailors' Home to get their opinions. Some thought a raft could make the journey easily, but no one wanted to join the adventure—not until Heyerdahl met an engineer named Herman Watzinger, the first man to sign up for the trip.

Watzinger and Heyerdahl worked as a team to solve problems, first of which was finding a crew. They quickly hired Knut Haugland and Torstein Raaby, both Norwegian radio engineers. Erik Hesselberg, a navigator, and others soon followed.

Then the U.S. Armed Forces agreed to support the trip if Heyerdahl and his crew would do some experiments for them. They wanted to test food provisions, such as knives, forks, and spoons that floated in water, a small stove, and other items.

Thor Heyerdahl needed to make sure he could build and safely sail a raft in South America. So he asked important Peruvian and Ecuadorian diplomats, who were located in New York City and Washington, D.C., for help.

Riding the Raft

To prove his theory, Heyerdahl wanted to construct a raft just like the one the primitive Peruvians would have used.

But how could he make such a raft? Heyerdahl found descriptions from fifteenth-century Spanish explorers. He also asked local peoples for help. Nothing modern was used, only natural materials from the area: nine long logs of balsa wood from Ecuador, banana leaves, bamboo mats, and twine ropes. When finished, the raft measured 45 feet by 18 feet.

Finding the needed balsa wood wasn't easy. Balsa wood grew in the rain forest, but when Heyerdahl and Watzinger arrived in Ecuador, it was the rainy season and no one was willing to go with them into the forest. The ground would be muddy and difficult to walk on, so they would need a jeep. Luckily, the president of Ecuador got them one. Once in the rain forest, they found and cut the logs. Then they floated them down the Rio Guayas to the Pacific Coast.

Balsa wood was very important to the design of the raft. This wood is very light and **buoyant,** and it floats like a cork on water. But it does have drawbacks. People warned Heyerdahl that the logs would gradually soak up water, grow heavier, and sink. Heyerdahl estimated that the trip would take at least ninety-seven days. Could the raft stay afloat for that long?

Naval experts also warned Heyerdahl that the ropes used to tie the raft together would rub against one another and grow weak and break, eventually causing the entire raft to fall apart!

The Kon-Tiki raft on the Pacific

Strong winds
caused trouble
for the raft.

The Beginning of the *Kon-Tiki* Journey

Despite all of the terrible warnings, the six men began their journey on the morning of April 28, 1947. A tugboat pulled the *Kon-Tiki* out of the Callao harbor in Peru and left the raft to drift with the winds and the currents.

Immediately, the sail filled with the trade wind, and the raft picked up speed and headed northwest. The crew had a hard time controlling the raft on stormy seas. For the first three days, they struggled to control the oar they used to steer, **situated** at the raft's stern. The violent waves kept them rolling, and steering the raft required two men at a time using their full strength. The job was so tiring that they had to schedule one-hour shifts. The *Kon-Tiki*'s crew worried that they would face this kind of work for the entire ninety-seven days!

During these frightening first days, the crew made certain that the men steering were tied to the raft with ropes. The violent waves could easily sweep them overboard with little chance of rescue. The raft was so small that it would seem **minuscule** in the vast ocean—hard for a plane or helicopter to spot, much less send out a rescue party.

Don't Always Believe What You're Told!

The stormy seas lasted for only a few days, but they proved that the raft was **seaworthy.** They also proved that the *Kon-Tiki* was just the right size. If the raft had been larger, it may have been snapped in half by the waves lifting up the bow or the stern.

The twine ropes didn't fray as experts warned. Instead, during the worst storms, they were protected by the balsa wood as they pushed into it. The logs were were tied loosely enough to move independently, which helped the raft ride the waves. It also allowed ocean water to flow through them, like soup through a fork.

Heyerdahl and his crew discovered that the raft was easy to steer because of the movable centerboards. By adjusting the depth and the angle of the centerboards, they conducted the raft steadily in whatever direction they chose.

Making Star Tracks

Although many navigational tools and instruments were available to Heyerdahl and his crew, they chose to use **celestial navigation.** This ancient system involves plotting a course using the sun and stars, just as the Peruvians would have done. Erik Hesselberg, the navigator, kept track of the raft's progress day by day. Like the Peruvians, Hesselberg noted the position of the sun during the day.

The parrot-fish constellation

Following a Sky Map

At night, Hesselberg used his knowledge of the stars, just as the South Americans and Polynesians had done in the past. Just as the Greeks had depended on the North Star, Orion, and other constellations to chart their course, Hesselberg looked for a group of stars shaped like a parrot fish and used its position in the sky to calculate their progress on the seas. Hesselberg measured the distance and direction the raft traveled each day, marking the point on a map. According to his measurements, they traveled an average of 42 miles a day.

Can you imagine embarking on a sea voyage, knowing that you would not set foot on land for more than three months? The men aboard the *Kon-Tiki* thought carefully about what cargo they brought on board. First, they had to pack food, medical supplies, extra materials for the raft, and fishing gear, necessary items that took up most of the space on the raft.

Packing Their Bags

The men didn't need extra clothes in the tropical heat, but there were other things they wanted aboard. Raaby and Haugland had to pack radio equipment and batteries. Hesselberg brought paints, brushes, and a guitar! Another crew member packed his box of books. The raft also carried plenty of film for recording their adventure.

Along with military food provisions, the *Kon-Tiki* carried coconuts, tropical fruit, dried meats, and lots of sweet potatoes, just as the original travelers might have prepared. Heyerdahl and his crew quickly learned that fishing was the easiest way to eat. In fact, flying fish flopped on board the raft all through the night. Whoever cooked the next morning would gather all of the fish on deck and prepare them for a meal. They even had enough that they used some of their night visitors as bait for bigger fish!

One night, Raaby, who slept closest to the cabin door, got frustrated by the night steersmen stepping on his hair. He put a lamp by his head—only to wake in the morning to the company of a snake mackerel!

Flying fish would "fly" onboard.

The crew of the *Kon-Tiki* found that they were never bored during their three months at sea. The fish were curious about the raft and not afraid of it, as they might have been if it had been a big ship.

A huge whale shark

Meeting and Greeting Ocean Fish

One night the crew noticed **phosphorescent** spots—light glowing beneath the ocean's surface. Often, different types of plankton would glow this way, but the spots seemed to cover one huge animal. In the morning, they saw the creature—a sixty-foot whale shark! The whale shark is the largest fish in the ocean, and its jaws can grow up to four feet wide. Although the shark swam around the raft for several hours, it never attacked the raft or the crew.

Smaller sharks, however, made the water dangerous for swimming. Once, while Haugland checked the bottom of the raft, a shark headed straight toward him! The men on board harpooned the shark to save Haugland from a nasty bite. By the end of the trip, the crew knew sharks so well that they could catch them by their tails!

The crew had more surprising night visitors. They would wake up to find baby octopi on the roof! At first they thought the octopi had crawled on board with their long tentacles. Then, one night, a strange thing landed on deck with a loud smack. An octopus had used its tentacles to jump through the water to escape a shark.

Safe Arrival

After three long months, the crew saw the first flock of birds they had seen since their departure. The men knew that land must be nearby. On their ninety-seventh day at sea—just as Heyerdahl had predicted—the crew spotted land. They were overjoyed at the sight and couldn't wait to feel the soft island sand between their toes. The *Kon-Tiki* had made it!

The wind, however, turned against them. It pushed the *Kon-Tiki* back out to sea. A few days later, they approached another island, Angatou. Two Polynesian men rowed a small canoe out of the dangerous coral reef to greet the boat, but there was no safe way to bring the *Kon-Tiki* to shore. They drifted out to sea again in despair.

The raft now headed straight for a **treacherous** reef. With no way around it, the crew prepared to go over it. They knocked out the centerboards and lashed their cargo tight to the raft. The *Kon-Tiki* bumped up against the reef, and wave after wave smashed against it. The men hung on to the ropes and stays with all their strength. The mast quivered, broke into pieces, and smashed into the cabin roof.

Finally, they made it to shore safely. At last they could stand on the reef in shoes—shoes they hadn't worn since they left Peru.

The rested crew of the *Kon-Tiki* arrives in San Francisco after their completed expedition.

The uninhabited island was named Kon-Tiki Island. Haugland and Raaby contacted Tahiti by radio with the news that they were safe ashore.

A Journey's End

After spending several weeks in the islands, meeting the Polynesians living there, the crew of the *Kon-Tiki* finally headed home. Had Thor Heyerdahl proved his theory? Even after publishing a book and making a film of his travels, he did not manage to convince all scientists worldwide. Thor Heyerdahl, however, had made the journey and had survived for many more adventures!

Now Try This

Navigating Your World

Could you be the captain of your own adventure? Explore the world around you! Use your navigation skills to go on your own adventure.

Before starting out, think of a place near your home that you would like to see and explore. You could go to a state park, a museum, or a historical site that interests you. Like Thor Heyerdahl, do your research first! Find out how to get there and write down clear directions. Will you need a car, a bus, a bicycle, or just your own two feet? Check the weather reports so you can plan what to wear. Find out the main attractions of your destination and make note of what you want to see there. Estimate how long your trip will take. Invite friends and family to come along!

1. First, plan what to bring as your cargo. Make sure that two of your items are a notebook and pen. What else do you need? You may need hiking boots, a flashlight, and some trail mix, or you may need your glasses and a camera. List the things you *need* to bring. Then list the items you *want* to bring. Do you have the space to bring everything?

2. When you're ready to go, assign roles to the friends and family who come along. You will need a navigator to keep track of the directions. Are there other jobs that would help you get to your destination safely?

3. On to the adventure! Make sure to jot down the interesting things you see and do in your notebook; this will be your Captain's Log. For each entry, write down the time and your location. When you return, the Log will help you share your journey with friends.

Glossary

buoyant *adj.* tending to float.

celestial *adj.* of or about the sky or outer space.

minuscule *adj.* extremely small.

navigation *n.* the process of finding and keeping a ship's or aircraft's position on course.

phosphorescent *adj.* giving out light without burning.

seaworthy *adj.* fit for sailing; able to stand storms at sea.

situated *adj.* placed; located.

treacherous *adj.* not reliable; deceiving.